Best wishes for
transformation

[signature]

Hardheaded
&
Softhearted

Hardheaded & Softhearted

Lessons from the Boardroom to the Break Room

Rick Belluzzo & Krish Dhanam

Brown Books Publishing Group
Dallas, Texas

Hardheaded & Softhearted
Lessons from the Boardroom to the Break Room

Brown Books Publishing Group
16250 Knoll Trail Drive, Suite 205
Dallas, Texas 75248
www.BrownBooks.com
(972) 381-0009

A New Era in Publishing™

ISBN 978-1-61254-126-6
LCCN 2013941022

Printed in the United States

10 9 8 7 6 5 4 3 2 1

For more information or to contact the authors, please go to www.SkyLifeSuccess.com

Dedicated to our fathers
Joseph Belluzzo and N. S. Dhanam

Two men who exemplified work ethic and whose stories
of rising from meager beginnings to prominent heights
in industry, community, and society have been the
inspiration for our journeys. Their commitments to the
premise that hard work pays and their love for family
have been visual examples of lives and legacies that are
now impacting the third and fourth generations.

Contents

Authors' Note

The "Hardheaded and Softhearted" phrase has come to mean so much to us and forms the basis for this collection of lessons and principles. We share the view that achieving long-term and sustained success in any endeavor requires the combination of delivering results—being hardheaded—and all of the human elements—being softhearted. Throughout life, we are confronted with these two elements, and success requires balance and optimization by achieving results while also sustaining the future. This is a lesson that seems to be forgotten in today's business and political environments. In both, we often see leaders pursue either end of the spectrum and miss the power of finding solutions to tough problems where Head and Heart come together.

As all of us face the challenges of navigating a path through an ever more complex and rapidly changing world, we must always strive to find the right balance between the head and the heart. Through this balance come success and satisfaction. As we wrote this book and chronicled these lessons, we wanted to highlight this core principle—where IQ meets EQ! The twenty-first century will no longer allow an "either-or" approach but demands an "and-also" approach.

Rick Belluzzo and Krish Dhanam

Chapter

1

Where IQ Meets EQ

In 1989, as a young, first-time Hewlett-Packard division general manager, I was presented with the biggest challenge and opportunity of my career. My recent promotion was probably the most significant of my life thus far, and I was charged with the task of continuing the momentum of HP's emerging laser printer business. This business was born in 1984 when, to the surprise of the industry, HP introduced the world's first desktop laser printer. HP quickly took the lead in this fast-growing market, and I, as a new division manager, was challenged with extending this lead or at a minimum protecting this enviable position. The pressure to deliver was intense. Of course I was very excited to have been given this opportunity, and yet I was clearly anxious about what steps I should take to achieve success.

The competition was growing, and we decided that to protect and extend our lead we needed to be the first company to introduce a laser printer that would break the $1,000 price barrier, a joke by today's standard but a major challenge in 1989. Our thinking was that we would expand the market to more price-sensitive segments and put the approaching competition back on their heels. The goal was $999—not $1,029 or $1,049, but under $1,000—no excuses.

This was a tough goal, but being the new leader, I took on the challenge with determination. This big move would make my mark in the industry and expand the success of this business. The priority was to deliver a cost structure to achieve this aggressive price goal. Very early we realized that we needed to secure an aggressive price for the underlying print engine, which was designed and manufactured by a long-standing partner in Japan. This partnership went back many years, and the mutual respect between the companies was golden.

With this aggressive goal established, I began the process of convincing our Japanese partner that we needed a lower price and that this would result in success for both companies. I took several trips to Japan and spent days negotiating, singing karaoke, and doing everything I could to make my case and convince our partner. Progress was slow, and the result still wasn't good enough. We were running out of time as the printer's introduction date approached. Finally the inevitable happened. I came home from the final trip and gave the bad news to our marketing team—we just couldn't get our cost low enough. We worked other aspects of the cost structure and still couldn't get there without our Japanese partner's agreement to make cost concessions. The marketing team was discouraged, and I felt I had failed to deliver. To say the least, I was frustrated.

With only a short time remaining, I decided that I could not accept my failure. I would give it one more try, so I convinced our Japanese partner to meet with me in Anchorage. I figured we would be on neutral territory, and I would make one last attempt to make my case. We were clearly out of time. This was my last chance.

We arrived on a Thursday night, had dinner, and worked on a solution all day Friday. After a day of discussion, we had made little progress, and I was prepared to return without a solution. I could not see how we could break the thousand-dollar barrier. Then, to my surprise, on Saturday morning as I was preparing to leave Anchorage, I received a call from our partner, who said, "Belluzzo-san, if you commit to higher volumes, we can meet your goal." Finally—the answer we needed. It seemed so simple.

The challenge was that their agreement required me to commit to volumes which were substantially above the marketing forecast. That was my new challenge. After some internal discussion, I decided to agree to the proposal, and I gave my commitment to this new pricing structure. I was very excited to have achieved this goal and to have the potential to extend our leadership.

Thirty days later, the product launched, the industry was astonished, and the competition was on their heels. The orders started to come in, and I had a strong sense of satisfaction and success. I felt pleased to make a difference and see the result.

My sense of fulfillment didn't last long. Within a few months, the inevitable problem began. The original marketing forecast was correct, and the production volumes that I committed to were exceeding sales. As a result, inventory levels were building at an alarming rate.

I can remember the day I flew to our major warehouse to see a portion of the over 350,000-unit inventory. I was stunned. As a new general manager, I was under incredible pressure to solve this problem. I pushed sales and marketing to implement aggressive sales programs, yet this was insufficient to solve a problem of this magnitude. I had no choice but to go back to our partner and reduce output, although I had given my commitment to this plan. This was an action I wanted to avoid at all costs, but I had to face the reality that there was no alternative.

I flew to Japan and started the process. I didn't have much time to solve the problem because the crisis was growing each day. That day was not my finest. I made my case and was told, "Belluzzo-san, you gave us your word." They were right. I had given my word, and yet we were all witnessing a growing crisis. My intentions were always to meet my commitment and make this a success for both companies.

After more rather humbling negotiation, finally we had a breakthrough—they agreed to reduce output for a small price adjustment. I accepted the offer and was ready to return home with a solution. Although this solution was a change in plans, I was sure we could continue to pursue our aggressive strategy. They understood the magnitude of the problem and were willing to take action to bail me out of this mess.

As I was leaving the conference room in Tokyo, they said, "Belluzzo-san, one more thing. We need you to travel to our factory in central Japan and meet with our team and all of our suppliers and accept your failure." At first I thought this was a joke, but joking was not part of the protocol. They were serious, and this request made me deeply internalize the impact of this issue that was of my doing.

I accepted the challenge and was on the bus the next morning. I soon found myself in front of thousands of people in a rural central Japan community, an entire community who had signed up for my commitment. I learned that my failure to deliver would impact all of them. This experience was sobering and humbling. I stood in front of the group in my dark suit, bowing and expressing my remorse and apology. I was accountable, and I personally accepted failure. This was a harsh lesson for me. I know it changed me forever. Now I can understand that I was so intent on achieving the goal that I didn't fully appreciate how my decision impacted a company, a community, and many lives.

The story ended well. The inventory cleared, the product was a grand success, and the long-standing relationship with a critical partner was preserved, maybe enhanced. We worked through a crisis together, found common ground, respected each other, aided a community, and succeeded in the marketplace.

This experience was the most graphic illustration of one of the most impactful pieces of advice I was ever given, when Dave Packard, cofounder of HP, once said, "To be a successful leader, you need to be hardheaded and softhearted."

This example was the ultimate of being hardheaded—solving a nasty problem and winning in the very competitive marketplace—and yet being softhearted, acknowledging my commitment and treating people with respect, while working to find a win-win solution. Although many people encouraged me simply to halt purchases and move on, I knew that there was more at stake, that I had given my word, and that trust was at the heart of this long-standing relationship. Thousands of people joined me in executing this aggressive plan. I had to make it right.

The other aspect of being hardheaded was practicing a powerful principle—Start from the Start. We must always begin grounded in a realistic perspective of the facts. In this case, I know I glossed over many points of reality and relied on hope and luck. The hardheaded principle taught me that before we can solve a problem, we must see it for what it is. We had a phrase at Microsoft that was something like "We need to wallow in the problem for a while." To be hardheaded, we must not create our own, more acceptable reality. If anything, we should err on the side of overstating the problem.

Hardheaded and Softhearted

1. Do you maintain the right balance between the short term and the long term?
2. If Hardheaded and Softhearted represented a continuum, are you operating in the optimum position?
3. How could you change your balance in order to become more effective?

"Coming together is a beginning;
keeping together is progress;
working together is success."

—Henry Ford

Chapter

2

Beginning Well: Say "Thank You"

The two words that have expressed gratitude for countless deeds and numerous actions are "thank you." They have conveyed heartfelt emotions and have been used to express genuine feelings. Sometimes they can patronize a person and at other times deflect a compliment. These two words are as commonplace as a sunrise or the air we breathe. Why then are these words so difficult to say? Why is offering genuine praise verbally so rare? Complimenting someone for a role in your success should not be hard. On the contrary, every environment should encourage verbal reward and recognition so that the culture is transformed by the expectation of gratitude.

I remember a time not too long ago when I was asked by one of my father's friends to make a speech at a local college in the city of my birth. It was a speech like any other, rehearsed and delivered in a way that had been done before. The difference was that it would be delivered in front of many people who knew my parents better than they knew me. I was caught up in the notoriety of my own accomplishments half a world away and was, I presume, putting on airs so I could impress my parents. In some way, I was seeking validation for what I had accomplished. My expectation for the moment was self-aggrandizement. Fred Smith Sr., a leadership luminary, said that we should not be swayed by the way we are introduced because the words of praise are mandatory. We should be touched by how people respond when we are done.

In organizations, people often leave disenchanted because they were never acknowledged for what they contributed. I had left my hometown many years earlier with the sentiment that no one there would appreciate me no matter what I did. I carried that burden until I met Mr. Zig Ziglar, the man who inspired me to embrace this principle of starting everything by saying "thank you."

My orchestrated opening for my speech that day was challenged, and what came out sounded like "Ladies and gentlemen," pause . . . "it gives me great pleasure to return home to Vizag. Thank you for the honor" pause . . . "Looking out at the students who are the leaders of tomorrow, I am humbled by the opportunity to address this august body" pause . . .

When the convulsions well up inside you, and the tears begin to form in the corners of your eyes, you know what is about to happen—first a wince, then a shuffle, followed by the adjustment of your notes and a glance away from the section that is causing you this discomfort. I looked again at my parents sitting in the front row. Mom was saying a silent prayer to protect her baby from bad luck, and Dad was beaming "That's my boy!"

"Thank you." It was all I could muster as I looked at those two wonderful people. "Thank you, Mom and Dad, for who you have allowed me to become. I dedicate this finest hour of my life, at the place where it all began, to you. I am a speaker now, but I have been your proud son all along." An hour of my speech elapsed, and I was done. The emcee asked my parents to stand and take a bow. He asked each student in the audience to set a goal to come back to the roots of their lives and thank their parents. My mama was crying, and my daddy was consoling her. Why had I waited so long to say "thank you"?

As I write this, I realize that those two people who had inspired so much in me never stopped growing. My mother is completing her master's degree in her seventies, and my father is beginning his doctoral studies a year shy of his eightieth birthday.

Don't wait to say thank you to the people who are the foundations of your life. The stress specialists all agree that gratitude is the healthiest of all human emotions. When we look at our organizations and teams, we must understand that hope without gratitude is hopelessness and change without strategy is cluelessness.

Where IQ Meets EQ

1. When was the last time you said "thank you" to your parents?

2. Who in your professional opinion is the most grateful person you know?

3. What specifically are you going to do tomorrow to showcase an attitude of gratitude?

"The person who seeks all their applause from outside has their happiness in another's keeping."

—**Dale Carnegie**

Chapter

3

Applause that Matters

Have you ever heard a story that just screamed the truth in such a way that it convinced you about your own errors? Have you ever heard an illustration that made a point so clear that you were sure about the conveyor's intent the moment it was revealed? Have you ever leaned forward during delivery of a message that was so compelling you knew that the speaker was brought there that day to deliver it to you? One such message was put forward by the late Adrian Rogers through his "Love Worth Finding" broadcasts.

The story is about a violinist who had just delivered a masterful performance. Every ounce of energy expended was rewarded with an ovation that was thunderous and long. The violinist retreated behind the stage curtains as the crowd, now standing, beckoned for him to take a bow. The handlers asked the maestro to go forward and take another bow. Gently, the violinist moved the drape of the curtain and pointed to a solitary, seated individual in the second row and said to the stagehand, "That man is not standing, and he is my teacher."

Have you ever been in a situation when you received accolades from everyone except the one whose admiration you craved? How many stories have we heard of organizations where the people who left said the primary reason was that they had not been recognized enough? Is a performance of a lifetime worth anything if the teacher does not applaud you? Have you ever found yourself on a team where you felt you were doing your best but were escaping the notice of those who determined your next promotion?

You and I are violinists in the orchestra of life, work, and responsibility. Our applause comes momentarily from task-related celebrations and projects whose deadlines have been met. Reports filed with meticulous detail are approved, and budgets are circulated for gleaming eyes to guess our importance by the size of our approvals. All this haste and busyness gives us the feeling of responsibility because we are all looking into the second row hoping our teacher will stand and applaud.

Many teachers in life will shortchange you and applaud you for your small deeds. Some teachers will never applaud you for any deed for fear that you might stop growing if they praise and acknowledge you. Others will sit and wait for the right moment to say to you "well done."

One of the men whom I admired deeply was the legendary motivator Zig Ziglar. I shared hundreds of flights with him as his associate, thus gaining a front-row seat to one who was best in his field. He always told me to be guarded against applause that might be construed as false praise.

Our environments and business cultures are being diminished because of political correctness. No longer is the applause meter set to genuine standards but seems to be lowered so that feelings will not get hurt. One of the fundamentals of a hardheaded and softhearted culture is the high standard of performance demanded before applause is doled out. Recognition fuels motivation, and reward propels achievement, but the applause that matters has to be genuine and usually reserved for those who performed by the rules.

Who are the teachers whose applause you seek? Has the race you have run been meaningful so far? Ask your family to search with you. You know that when the student is ready, the teacher will appear.

Hardheaded and Softhearted

1. What are you going to do to applaud someone in your personal life?
2. What are you doing to encourage someone in your professional life?
3. Who is the person in your organization who is the most generous with applause?

"When we are no longer able
to change a situation, we are
challenged to change ourselves."

—Viktor Frankl

Chapter

4

Thriving on Disruption

Over the last decade, we have witnessed an accelerating rate of change that has cut across virtually every aspect of our economy. Having worked in technology my entire career, I thought I had become accustomed to rapid changes that had the potential to alter the future of companies. The new reality is that extreme change is occurring at breakneck speed, touching all our lives and businesses. There is no place to hide or avoid the impact of this change.

I can remember one cold winter day shortly after becoming the CEO of Quantum Corporation, at the time the leader in the development of data tape drives used to protect information. I visited our development team in Boulder, Colorado. We gathered in one large room, and I gazed at one of the largest and most capable tape drive engineering teams in the world. That day we had to discuss the harsh reality that the market for tape drives was declining at a rapid rate because they were being replaced by new technologies. The harsh reality was that the world was going to need fewer tape drive engineers and that, for these people, work would not be the same. That was a graphic example that these rapid changes were disrupting not only companies but also the lives of people and their families.

Never before in our history have we seen the forces of new technology, globalization, new business models, and new competition reshape our world in positive ways and also force change in our lives, careers, and livelihoods. These forces have led to insecurity and uncertainty. The notion of a "recession" in our economy is an outdated concept, since the real impact on our livelihood is more about change and disruption caused by these macro forces than simply by fluctuations in economic activity.

We must remember that even in these times of uncertainty opportunities are flourishing in areas that are "on the right side of gravity." Businesses and fields that are beneficiaries of change, products that are in strong demand, innovations in business models, and other outcomes can benefit from these forces. There is a new world of opportunity behind the harsh restructuring that surrounds us.

One aspect of human nature is to strive for stability and find comfort, but the forces around us are challenging our preference for the status quo. Resisting this trend is counterproductive. Many companies and individuals fail simply because the prospects of change are so daunting that they find comfort in doing everything possible to define the world in a more convenient model. All resisting change does is delay the pursuit of a set of actions that can be responsive to the inevitable forces of change. So embrace the start from the start principle—embrace the changes and define the challenge as it really is. Then you can start to find new ideas, new energy, and new hope.

The first sign of responding to this new world order is to become a person who looks at the world in a new way. The most successful people I know tend always to be out in front, enthusiastically looking for change. Instead of fighting the trends, they embrace them and look for opportunity. A renewed attitude and approach are vital. It is important to avoid complaining and feeling like a victim. Then you can become a person who looks for the "upside" of every situation. This step is the first toward being a person who can thrive on disruption.

Where IQ Meets EQ

1. What is your biggest fear?
2. If this fear were to occur, what good thing COULD happen?
3. Where might you be overly optimistic? Are there areas where you need to make an adjustment?

"Vanity and pride are different
things, though the words are often
used synonymously. A person may
be proud without being vain. Pride
relates more to our opinion of
ourselves; vanity, to what we
would have others think of us."

—Jane Austen

Chapter
5

Love Being the Underdog

Have you ever been patronized? Have you ever been told that you were the right person for the job, only to be told that someone else was getting it because that applicant had a little "extra"? Have you at any time in the course of your professional journey wondered if you were going to get the break?

Success as a commodity is always going to have standards that seem arbitrary; however, when you look at personal and professional achievement as a journey with a destination, the rules become different. Nobody loves being the underdog, but the premise of the principle is trying to find the common ground, and propels the mind to look for solutions. Some of the solutions are actually glimpses into what does not work in one instance but delivers for another. An underdog is always learning to add to a personal arsenal of beliefs in order to move ahead in the race.

In business, we encounter certain examples of performance that just stand out in our minds and stay with us over a period of time. Early in my career of working with the Zig Ziglar organization, I was entrusted with the opportunity to expand the international business. Granted, the reputation of Mr. Ziglar had already reached the status of legend, and many people wanted to be considered vendors and partners mostly for the regard they received when they advertised our name as one of their clients. The organization used a lot of speakers and consultants to travel domestically, and that side of the business was already firmly established with one vendor. Change would be a long process. Knowing the international business that I would represent would be a fraction of the travel budget of the organization, a lot of people were still vying for it. During this time, I was privileged to engage the services of Skypass Travel for these limited international trips. The recommendation from a friend about the company's reputation was the reason for the choice.

The CEO of the company, Victor Abraham, treated me with true pride for what I had done as a person from India trying to make a mark in the seminar business. He never really cared about the dollar amount of any specific transaction with me. He was always extra gracious, lifting me up with the assurance that if there was anything he could do to further my own pursuits, he would do it if I only asked. I am embarrassed to count the number of times he came through on his promise but thrilled that, after almost fifteen years, today we work as business partners globally. As you build your reputation with your vendors and clients, do it with genuine pride for the relationship instead of false praise for the benefit.

- **False praise** is, in the eyes of the one being affected, an assault on innocence. In the jungle that is a corporation and in the mayhem that is daily activity, people who spend their time praising others for reasons other than genuine concern are missing the point.

There is a dearth of real recognition in the world as people with huge holes in their hearts traverse through the maze of productivity, hoping that someone will take a real interest in them. Before I ask you for a gut-check, I am holding my own hand high so as to be honest with myself for having participated in the ritual of false praise. Sometimes we do it to belong, and sometimes we do it to feel good, but in most cases it is a mask that hides something deeper.

- **Reiterating your commitment** should not include a rendition of your own personal misery. Sometimes we hide our comments behind our own stories so that we can validate our choices. On a recent engagement, I found myself curled up on the back seat of a sedan for an all-night drive because of a canceled flight. I must tell you that informing everyone of my plight was not so much so that they would understand my predicament. I did it so I could claim martyrdom in the cut-throat, winner-take-all arena of motivational speaking. If you are committed, quit acting like a martyr, because all suffering is personal and not relative. Trying to reduce everything to the point of how much it costs is very human. Culture transformation begins when individuals and institutions focus on commitment proactively and not reactively. Every organization that succeeds pays a price, but the majority of them that enjoy the victory take three actions:

- They change their vocabulary to reflect not that they paid the price but that they enjoy the benefits.
- The system has the chronology of success displayed and does not showcase their mistakes for public consumption.
- Everyone in the culture is fully ingrained in the positive traits that make up the story of success.

- **Genuine gratitude for opportunity** should have no caveats. You either believe in everything you are doing, or you don't. Don't be partially grateful for some of the things that please you and complain about the things that benefit others. The healthy image that gratitude gives you is liberating. I remember that on a recent speaking tour of Asia my friend and coauthor Rick Belluzzo reminded me during one of my rants that we were privileged in that we were taught well. How simple to be grateful for the inputs in your life.

  Building your reputation on genuine pride and gratitude lets you take advantage of situations in which you are considered by some to be the "underdog" but which, in reality, merely pay tribute to your lack of vanity.

Hardheaded and Softhearted

1. Identify three steps that will assist you in simplifying your commitment.

2. Who are the most committed people you know in your immediate family? Why do you think they have been able to succeed within the same environment?

3. If you are a small business owner, do you have a "wall of gratitude" that showcases your successes? What are you grateful for when you reflect on each of those moments?

"Each problem has hidden in it an opportunity so powerful that it literally dwarfs the problem. The greatest success stories were created by people who recognized a problem and turned it into an opportunity."

—**Joseph Sugarman**

Chapter

6

A Good Crisis Is a Terrible
Opportunity to Waste

If there is one lesson I have learned working in the technology industry for nearly forty years, it is that disruption is "the mother of opportunity." With every innovative new technology or new business model, new leaders are created, and established leaders are threatened.

In the early 1980s, I was working in the printer business for Hewlett-Packard in Boise, Idaho. We were struggling, competing with a number of Japanese companies in a printer market that was dominated by a technology called "impact" printers—the ones that made the irritating noise. We were doing all we could to catch up but failed to make any measurable progress. Then a new idea emerged. There was a disruption coming called "non-impact" printing, a series of new technologies. We decided to leave our miserable existence behind and make a "big bet" on this disruption.

In 1984, we introduced the world's first ink jet printer and the world's first desktop laser printer—non-impact technologies. The rest is history. HP quickly became the market leader and eventually held more than 50 percent market share. The leaders of the old technology failed to make the transition. I am confident that the genesis of the big move came out of frustration and dissatisfaction with the status quo.

I often wonder if the outcome would have been different had we been a viable contender in the established printer market. There is no doubt that our struggles motivated us to find a new path that allowed us greater advantage. It made taking the risk much easier. This is one of the most significant leadership challenges that we can face—leading an organization to change and take risk, even when things seem fine.

Early in my executive career at HP, I was managing a series of divisions and I, along with others, felt that one division in particular was heading for a difficult transition and set of challenges. The leadership team was not moving fast enough to avoid the future peril. I was having lunch with my mentor one day and told him about my difficulty. I explained that the team was resistant to changing strategy because the current state of the business was good enough. He said to me, "Well, if there isn't a crisis yet, maybe you should create one." He was an avid student of history and was aware that empires failed because of a tradition of success.

I proceeded to take his advice and soon implemented a series of actions that turned the team's world upside down. This promoted aggressive change and the creation of an extremely successful line of new products. The advice had worked but reinforced the fact that embracing disruption is not an easy task for a business or an individual, yet embracing disruption is essential to success.

This lesson of embracing disruption is repeated over and over. In fact, today there are numerous examples of major disruptions creating a new industry leader and severely damaging the incumbent. I am sure we can all list many examples that touch our lives every day. This business lesson also applies to our lives and careers. Our businesses, occupations, and investments are all being impacted by disruption and change. We need to have our own personal strategic plan for our career, just as we did at HP almost thirty years ago. We need to look for the disruptions that threaten us and those that create opportunity.

One certainty is that we also have to be willing to consider "nontraditional" ideas. Sometimes this means suspending disbelief, changing our view of "what is possible," and not accepting no as an answer. Certainly my career is an example of taking an unusual path and rejecting the advice of my high school guidance counselor, who suggested I bypass college and go straight to trade school. I "wasn't college material."

Disruption can create new opportunities to build a new business, develop a new skill, start a new career, or make a bet on change. We need to be looking for these opportunities not only when times are tough but especially when things seem fine.

Where IQ Meets EQ

1. What do you see as some of the biggest disruptions that impact your career?
2. What can you do to take advantage of these disruptions if you have no limitations?
3. What are the barriers that prevent you from acting? Are they really insurmountable?

"I was dyslexic; I had no
understanding of schoolwork
whatsoever. I certainly would have
failed IQ tests. And it was one of
the reasons I left school when I was
15 years old. And if I—if I'm not
interested in something, I don't
grasp it."

—**Richard Branson**

Chapter

7

Compete and Complete

As you go about your daily business, you have probably noticed that people seem to be obsessed with puzzles. Sudoku, crosswords, Daily Jumble, Scrabble, and Words with Friends have evolved into a new kind of addiction. Commuters on trains and planes spend a lot of them deciphering solutions while keeping their minds occupied. This addiction may have two components. One is to tease the brain to be constantly challenged, and the other is to stay connected to something that really does not judge you when you fail. The second component is probably more important in modern cultures, since pages that contain unfinished or erroneously filled-in puzzles are commonplace.

We have slowly evolved into a group that likes the challenge but frowns on the evaluation. Schools are trying to find ways to grade students on the curve. Academic activism is suggesting "creative spelling" to ensure that certain segments of the population are not disenfranchised. What would leaders like Vince Lombardi, Harry Truman, George Patton, and Winston Churchill have said to the approach of being incomplete while demanding a fair grade? Sports have reduced themselves to clichés like "it is not whether you win or lose; it is how you play the game."

As a result, organizations have also been forced to adapt to this structure of catering to habits and behaviors that are byproducts of those thought processes. What seems like an innocent leveling of the playing field actually fosters a lack of competition. Not everything has to be a contest, but finishing that which challenges us should be paramount in any environment.

When I arrived in America at the age of twenty-four, I quickly found myself victimized by broader society. As an immigrant, I was expected to be a second-class citizen, and my habits and behaviors were dictated by staying with others similar to me. It was comforting to be nurtured by the citizens of my own homeland who had created an association that reflected the values of the country we had left. There was no real incentive to integrate into new beliefs that warranted change in language, enunciation, and pronunciation.

In the years since, I have observed entire cultures lowering their expectation so that they would not be perceived as exclusionary. My father, who had to abandon many of his own choices because of obligations, has said to me repeatedly that for every step I took in life, he would take one right behind me. If I were ever to fall, he would be right there to catch me. That instilled in me a feeling that I may not win at everything but that the goal of the game is to compete and complete. We need to encourage behavior to show that failure is an event and that it will never be a person. We need to foster an environment where the art of participation and playing is encouraged so that "winning" and not "whining" become commonplace.

At a sales meeting early in my career, I was taxed for the answers that I needed to some of the questions being posed to me. They were not easily accessible on a solutions page, and no one seemed to care that I was struggling. As a sales manager, I made it my mission always to offer help before a problem existed. That gave people in my department the confidence that the culture we were creating allowed mistakes but that participation and trying were not optional.

I now realize that many such moments exist in the career of a professional where people choose the easy way out, not trying because then they do not have to be evaluated. Fred Smith Sr. often said that if a man tries to get by in life without errors, he is akin to the outfielder who does not try for the hard ones and simply lets them go.

Sometimes in the pursuit of our professional roles, we develop habits and behaviors that address the overt but ignore the covert. If your exterior is polished and the clothes that cover you spell success, look inside and see if there are any anxieties caused by familial separation, lackluster parenting, a loose tongue, or haphazard matrimony.

Do you need to change any behaviors that are the results of erroneous habits? Do you want the clues to become simple again and the outcome a little more predictable? Why can we not earn a living and balance a life in the same pursuit? Can we really win it all by winning both personally and professionally? Is there one set of skills that, when we make them habitual, will give us the formula for total success?

Be grateful for the opportunities you have, for many do not have them. When you lament your situation, be thankful that you were chosen to do a task that is considered difficult. By embracing the unique nature of your challenge, you will seek and eventually find the answers that will allow you to solve the problems in your path. Ironically most people like to remain in problem mode so that they can blame the organization, the policies, and maybe even the predecessor in that job. This happens at the departmental, organizational, and national level. Changing the behavior and habits that caused the problem might be the best solution for the problem at hand.

Hardheaded and Softhearted

1. Which of your behaviors is your biggest weakness on the job?
2. How are you going to change the way you grade unacceptable behavior?
3. What new skills will you learn to create new habits and new behaviors?

"So that the record of history is absolutely crystal clear, there is no alternative way, so far discovered, of improving the lot of the ordinary people that can hold a candle to the productive activities that are unleashed by a free enterprise system."

—Milton Friedman

Chapter
8

You Are the Enterprise

Today's employment world is different from the one that our parents and grandparents enjoyed. There used to be a sense of security and belief that we could gain a skill or degree, join a large firm, do a good job, and know that there was security—and opportunity. Of course, today is different. The rate of change in the environment almost guarantees that we will have to re-invent ourselves a few times in our career. The value of the work we do is changing, we are living longer, and companies no longer can see a way to provide a sense of security. We must take a new approach.

In today's environment, all should recognize that "YOU are the enterprise." We must all think of ourselves as entities that must be competitive. We must strive to become more valuable—learn new skills, build relationships, establish a network. In fact, building multiple sources of income in order to maximize our potential and protect ourselves from negative events is becoming increasingly common. You and I must be more valuable enterprises that can transition, change, and adapt.

This is the best way I know to ensure ongoing success and purpose. Never get stale and never get comfortable. No company survives by standing still, and that is also true of people. So take that class, pursue that passion, build that website, start that business, and reach out to establish contacts and relationships.

Those who embrace this principle will find that many changes are underway that make building greater value in YOUR enterprise much easier. New technology, social networking, and online resources can allow each of us to pursue new horizons and revitalize our sense of opportunity.

Recently I was invited to come to Italy to give a speech to a "start-up" conference of young entrepreneurs. All the economic news for Southern Europe was bleak, and the popular press painted a picture of despair for young people, with staggering unemployment for those in their twenties. This group must have not read the news.

I arrived at the conference in Milan not knowing what to expect. What I found was an energetic group of young people with passion to build something new. They were clear about how their innovation would change the world, and they were determined to succeed. They were small teams, but using the power of mobile computing and other tools, they were able to start companies and gain traction with minimal investment. They were successful examples of people who understand that building an enterprise around their energy and skills is their path forward.

Since our career is a journey, we need to remember that we are all likely to face a number of significant transitions. These are times where our jobs come to an end, we move, or we have children. Times of transition are often disorienting, and we can easily get frozen. These transitions can be the most significant events of our lives. We can make the most important decisions during these times and should approach them with energy and optimism.

One of the best pieces of advice I was given when I left Microsoft was to talk to as many people as I could, get advice, listen to ideas, talk to more people, and not make any quick decisions. I took this advice and approached the transition as if it were my job. I was up every day working the process and then waiting for the right time to decide what was next for me. Transitions are big, confusing, and critical times. Take them on with purpose and joy.

Where IQ Meets EQ

1. What makes you valuable as an enterprise?

2. What is your list of actions to make your enterprise more valuable?

3. Are you in a transition now? How could you get the most out of it?

"The greatest achievement was
at first and for a time a dream.
The oak sleeps in the acorn, the
bird waits in the egg, and in
the highest vision of the soul a
waking angel stirs. Dreams are
the seedlings of realities."

—**James Allen**

Chapter

9

Textbooks for Father and Son

I vividly remember when my childhood dream of being at Oxford came true. I was attending a summer school event conducted by the famed apologist Dr. Ravi Zacharias and his team. These carefully accented teachers had a hint of the glory that was England and the subsequent reformation that allowed a new world to be discovered alongside man's ambition. Prime ministers who reported for duty amid the grandeur of a monarchy seemed immortalized in canvas alongside the authors of repute who wrote in the same tavern. Oxford is a true glimpse into a past that shaped a future. Though my formal education had finished over two decades prior to this experience, I still experience a thrill when I think of those two summers when I was fortunate to live out the vision that began as fantasy.

We are never too young to start learning and never too old to relearn. My seventy-nine-year-old father, who just finished his master's degree at seventy-seven, has enrolled in a local university in India to begin work on his doctoral studies. When he was reminded that he would be in his eighties when he finishes his PhD, he responded by asking how old would he be if he did not try. The issue at hand was not the degree or the attempt. His statement inspires me: "When my obligations in this life finished, I still had an obligation to my dreams." Today I have the rare privilege of buying my son and my father textbooks at the same time. That was not one of the dreams I had as a child but a true benefit of being focused, having a vision, and pursuing the steps required to fulfill it diligently.

Early in my career at the Zig Ziglar Corporation, I saw in its leader a man whose appetite for new information was transcended only by his desire to ensure that others had the same opportunity to learn. For a number of years, he bought me a copy of every book that he thought would be beneficial to me. They would just be waiting on my desk or in my inbox. The privilege we have in the sheer abundance of information waiting to be grasped is indeed awesome. No matter how modern we think our journey is, and no matter how ancient we think some advice is, we need to be the catalysts that fuse these eras so we can be productive in our collective output.

My good friend Victor Abraham gave me three principles of fulfilling a vision:

1. Be grateful for the nightmares caused by mistakes because they teach you how to dream better. Problems produce patience, and patience produces perseverance. While nobody prays for problems, almost everyone in business who has weathered a storm uses the storm as a lesson during the calm.

2. The difference between an amateur and a professional is that an amateur looks at everything as a gamble while a professional assesses everything as a calculated risk. This does not mean that a professional will win every time, but having the vision to know the difference between a gamble and a risk is the difference between status quo and progress.

3. Always use your strengths in negotiation so that the other party cannot exploit your weaknesses. I never understood the genius behind this principle until I moved personally from being an employee to a business owner. The first series of negotiations was done with a poor vision that was based on my limited understanding of business because I had always worked for someone else. When I chose to work for myself, I did not realize the strength I brought to the table by having a solid team alongside me that was strong in all the areas in which I was deficient.

The logic behind the pursuit of a carefully planned vision is in seeing everything through the lens of experience.

Hardheaded and Softhearted

1. Who will you impact this year so that you are passing on what you know?
2. Where in your past will you look for the advice that might help the present?
3. Who among your family and friends can you lean on so that your learning is complete and inclusive of other points of view?

"And, of course, method is very important as is a high-quality specialist (trainer) working with you to keep you going in the right direction for your improvement and to help create results."

—**Sergei Bubka**

Chapter

10

The 80/20 Rule

Make no mistake: in a competitive world, delivering results and being considered a solid performer are essential elements to success. I have told my two sons that they should pursue whatever career and profession they are passionate about. The only thing to consider is the 80/20 rule—20 percent of the individuals in any field achieve 80 percent of the success, 80 percent of the income, and 80 percent of the recognition. As long as they strive to be part of the top 20 percent, they can achieve distinction and success.

In this very competitive world, we should enter a field, start a business, or pursue a goal only if we are committed to be in the top 20 percent. Setting our personal goals higher than the norm is the first step towards achieving distinction and success. This approach makes us think differently and create the energy to achieve great things. What we do is important, but how we do it is what makes us unique, different, and valued.

I try to remind myself of a few practices that have helped me exceed expectations.

- **The right commitments:** I have always been a believer in under-promising and over-delivering. Make sure you commit to a successful outcome, but leave room to do better. Being known as a person who always gets the job done is a characteristic of a top 20 percent performer. Success breeds success, and building a culture of winning created around exceeding commitments is important.

- **Sense of urgency:** Time is always a scarce commodity. Don't waste a moment as you work toward achieving a goal or responding to a request. Being first to achieve a goal almost always yields disproportionate benefits.

- **Focus on the critical few:** As I start each week, I make a list of all of the goals that I want to achieve. Then I quickly narrow that list to the essential tasks that will make the greatest impact on achieving my goals. I have always noted that successful CEOs have a clear view of the factors that will have the greatest impact and the courage to let the other things move at a slower rate.

- **Attention to detail:** Have pride in your work— there isn't room for a halfhearted effort. Accept a task only if you are willing to provide the focus and effort to meet your personal standard. Look for opportunities to do something special.

- **Accountability:** I once heard another CEO say, "When something goes wrong in my company, I start with the point of view that it's my fault." When you fall short, own it—don't defend your shortfall. I once had a board member tell me, "Rick, you are really hard on yourself." I have always preferred to be hard on myself rather than have my boss be hard on me.

In the end, results and performance matter. We see that every day in sports, business, and virtually every other aspect of life. Make the pledge to be a top performer by making the right commitment, pursuing it with energy, staying focused on what matters, being proud of your work, and accepting any shortfall.

Where IQ Meets EQ

1. In what area do you want to achieve distinction?
2. How do you measure success?
3. What do you need to do differently to improve?

"The unselfish effort to bring cheer
to others will be the beginning of a
happier life for us."

—**Helen Keller**

Chapter

11

One Size Does Not Fit All Mentors

An apparent consistency in business is the need for role models and mentors. Almost everywhere the art of self-improvement and corporate advancement is tied closely to the need to have mentors or guides. Seeking help from others and creating opportunities for constructive criticism is a proven plan for reaching important milestones.

The question that confronts us all is not whether we need role models but whether the role models we choose are consistent in their own lives. Sometimes the charisma of the messenger clouds our judgment, and we settle for the wrong conduits of information. The skeptical nature of humanity has created a unique problem because we want solutions that are perfect and usually trust individuals who are imperfect with the task of providing us these solutions.

On a recent television program, a popular talk show host and a champion of countless causes was exposed after giving a platform to someone who by all subsequent revelations turned out to be a fraud. Since her good reputation over a period of time far outweighed this one mistake, the world moved on. My business and spiritual mentor, Zig Ziglar, who was the most consistent man I know, said that a father who tells his son not to speed but uses a radar detector is actually telling his child that breaking the law is a crime but not getting caught is genius. When you choose role models, look for consistency in all they do.

Corporate philosophies are not exempt from the need for consistency. I recently had the opportunity to talk to a group of internal auditors of colleges and universities on the subject of ethics. The issue was not whether there was a need for ethics—the problem was the tag of "relativism" attached to ethics. If we teach ethics in an abstract way in our business schools, then why are we surprised when a WorldCom or an Enron grabs the headlines? Companies that talk a good game and never practice what they preach are like the boy who cried wolf. The timeless relevance of any message is tied to its consistency. The true meaning of consistency is revealed in the message itself.

Ensure that your mentors and role models in business are people who are capable of deciphering the real meaning of a task or the real purpose of an objective. If you are the owner of a philosophy or the moderator of a message, try to get out of the way of interpretation and let the message shine through you.

People who cannot stand behind the talents of their own accomplishments usually seek refuge behind the warped translation of another's legacy. In the field of mentoring, whether you choose to become one due to your accomplishments or whether you are seeking one for progress, ensure that you are thorough in your research. Mentoring cannot be achieved through proxy or affiliation. Just because someone's father was great does not mean that the progeny is automatically gifted in the same category as the father. By the same token, your title and job responsibility do not qualify you to be an expert on anything other than your title and job description.

Remember that mentoring is a privilege because you shape another life by sharing those experiences. Ensure that you do not pick one person to be your mentor in everything. I have spiritual mentors who guide me on my personal needs; business mentors like my coauthor Rick, whom I call on for everything pertaining to business because that is his forte; and I have relationship advisors. The key is realizing the need for guidance and then strategically finding the people who can provide expertise.

The spirit of renewal comes with every New Year. The desire to be different is reborn on January 1. Resolutions are made, and disciplines are sought. This year make a decision to wish everyone a Happy Year so that renewal and rebirth take place on whichever day you choose to be the first day of the next 365. In the words of Fred Smith Sr., "Every great teacher is looking for a great student. Become a great student to a great teacher."

Hardheaded and Softhearted

1. Do you choose those who influence your life based on the consistency of how they live their own?

2. Who are some students you are going to impact?

3. What are you doing to find new teachers?

"Virtually every company will be going out and empowering their workers with a certain set of tools, and the big difference in how much value is received from that will be how much the company steps back and really thinks through their business processes . . . thinking through how their business can change, how their project management, their customer feedback, their planning cycles can be quite different than they ever were before."

—Bill Gates

Chapter
12

Did YOU Cause the Mutiny?

The most valuable development tool we have is the feedback we receive from our surroundings. This is true in all aspects of life and especially in our professional and business endeavors. Every interaction has some element of feedback that can make us better and improve our product, service, and business.

I learned a very tough lesson early in my career. I was fortunate to have been promoted to supervisor early in my tenure at Hewlett-Packard. I was young and as high as a kite. I was ready to be the best leader possible, get the best results, and do whatever necessary to be a success. What happened next was something that I didn't think was possible.

My work group—all eight people—revolted. They all went to my manager and said I was impossible—a terrible supervisor. This devastated me. It seemed to happen suddenly, and I was at a loss to know what to do next. After a sleepless night, I returned to the office, met with my manager, and asked for another chance. He allowed me this opportunity. I immediately sat down with my work group and listened to what they had to say. I developed a plan to improve and got that second chance. The lesson was that I was oblivious to my surroundings.

My team was providing me critical feedback that I had missed. I learned lessons from that event that would help me avoid being oblivious ever again.

1. Be keenly aware of feedback—good and bad.
2. Make it easy for people to tell you what you might not want to hear.
3. Take responsibility for your personal development plan.

4. Avoid being defensive or people will "shut down."

5. Criticism is a good thing—even if wrong.

All of these boil down to being self-aware, knowing your weaknesses, and catching yourself in mistakes. Soon you won't be making those mistakes. You need practice and learning to avoid the common errors. One of the best compliments you can receive is "being open"—open to hearing new ideas, open to hearing difficult feedback, open to bad news. Responding and improving under our own direction is empowering.

This principle also applies to your business. I have always been amazed by companies who shun customer feedback. Often they seem more interested in arguing than learning from the experience. Since I have spent my career in the technology business, I have too many stories of companies that implemented a solution that fell short of the customer's needs. Nothing can be more defeating than winning an opportunity and then failing during the implementation.

I remember one time when I was asked by a global bank customer to come to London to discuss a project. I energetically jumped on a plane for the eleven-hour flight, thinking this early project would be expanded to their entire network. Instead the customer expressed dissatisfaction and lack of interest in doing more business. I was devastated and frustrated beyond belief. I have always prided myself in my ability to take the harsh medicine and respond in a professional way with the objective to learn and get a second chance.

I accepted the "firing" with as much class as I could, having traveled halfway around the world to get the news. But it also allowed me to replay the series of events and see all the signs and subtle feedback. It was a difficult lesson that again reinforced how feedback is all around us and essential to becoming better at what we do.

Where IQ Meets EQ

1. Whose feedback is important to you?
2. Do they feel free to give you that feedback? If not, what changes do you need to make?

3. What is your personal plan for being more self-aware, catching your mistakes, and practicing being open to feedback?

"If you don't make a total commitment to whatever you're doing, then you start looking to bail out the first time the boat starts leaking. It's tough enough getting that boat to shore with everybody rowing, let alone when a guy stands up and starts putting his life jacket on."

—**Lou Holtz**

Chapter

13

Did the Child Give All Her Candy?

Apreacher from India once told a story that I paraphrase. There was a boy who had a collection of marbles that were his pride and joy. They were big and little, colorful and shiny, and the envy of all the kids he played with. He had inherited most of them from his older brother who had taken extremely good care of them. There was a also girl who had a lot of candy and had saved her allowance every week to invest in her growing stock. She always carried a small supply during playtime but was careful always to add to her inventory because she never wanted to run out. One day the boy and the girl decided to make a deal. She would give him all her candy if he gave her all the marbles.

The girl brought all the candy to the point of exchange and met the boy, who produced his marbles. All the marbles were there except the most prized ones, which he had carefully separated and hidden. The boy and the girl exchanged their glorious collections and went their separate ways. That night the girl slept blissfully as she marveled at her new possession and was thankful for her treasure. The boy lay awake, wondering if she had given him all the candy or if she had held some back, just as he had.

There comes a time in all our lives when we tire of what we know and trade for what someone else has that we think is more valuable. Do you stay awake at night wondering if you have given your all? Have you ever held back just enough for yourself in case the going got tough? Whom have you bartered with in the journey of life that actually received less than they deserved but gave you more than they could afford?

Many a relationship grows stale as employers and employees claim they have given their all while secretly holding back just the right amount to sustain them in case of peril. Many teammates walk away from the team when they see signs that the credit for success is going to someone else. They then hold back and say to themselves that the threat really doesn't matter because they are small pawns in a gigantic chess game.

We are all victims of this saga that convinces us that we do not need to give it our all because, in the grand scheme of living, no one will ever know the difference. The sleepless nights and restless moments do not trouble the people who are fully committed. They usually create consternation for the one who knows that he or she could have given more. To succeed, there is a level of risk involved in committing your full capabilities. Sometimes you have to do everything just to belong. There was a time when I realized that I did not have all the qualifications to belong to a team. The advice from my counterparts was to wait my turn. I realized that the only way I would learn would be to make an effort to be as close to the activity as possible and hope that eventually the peripheral knowledge I acquired would at least be enough to put me on the bench. Your odds of being utilized are better when you are on the bench than they are if you are in the stands.

- Give more than you have to the commitments you made when you were chosen to belong.
- Don't participate only when you have something to spare from your protection.
- Willfully pledge your all to those around you and make sacrifice a priority.

You will soon learn that happiness depends on happenings but that the unadulterated joy of living comes from giving your all.

Hardheaded and Softhearted

1. Corral someone you know and love and give your undivided attention while focusing on solving that person's problems.
2. Make a list of the opportunities you had this week to give a little more but held back because

you were waiting for something that will not come.

3. What are you holding back on a daily basis that is preventing you from achieving stardom?

"The person who makes a success
of living is the one who sees
his goal steadily and aims for it
unswervingly. That is dedication."

—Cecil B. DeMille

Chapter

14

Make a Difference . . .
Every Minute, Every Day

In today's hyper-competitive world, no opportunity to build advantage can be missed. This principle is true whether it applies to a business or to individuals. Each and every day we have a unique opportunity to conduct our lives with distinction or mediocrity. There should be no room for mediocrity. The basic point is that each and every task, interaction with a person, or moment we live represents a chance to do it better than anyone else. This is what making a difference is all about—living life believing that we all have countless opportunities each day to demonstrate our value, to be unique, and to leave our business, family, church, community, friends, and even total strangers better off because we decided to make a difference. Every day becomes a rich experience, never boring and always impactful.

One evening I was connecting through Chicago to return to my home in Boise. There were weather problems, and flight schedules were a mess. I remember seeing an elderly couple wandering the gate area, looking very confused. I approached them and asked if I could help. They couldn't speak a word of English but handed me a piece of paper with a phone number on it. I called that number and spoke to their son. They were coming to visit Boise from a small village in Eastern Europe. They had never flown before; in fact, they had never left the village. The son had lost contact with them and was worried. I ended up escorting them to their family in Boise to cheers and immense gratitude. What a gift that was for me, and a deep lesson that we can be better in business and in every aspect of life by looking for opportunities to make a difference. Given the stress of a long week and travel problems, I could have moved on. Instead, I made the decision to make a difference.

A business leader gave me some very good advice: "Never pass a problem unattended." This is all about attention to detail and making everything you touch better than before. It means never being complacent about the life we live or the work we do and not procrastinating. Problems don't solve themselves.

I learned this concept when I started my career at Hewlett-Packard and immediately recognized that my experience and education were well below the norm in my workgroup. I was younger and less educated than everyone else in my department. At first, I felt very insecure, but I quickly turned this into an advantage. The lesson of my father, an Italian immigrant who could not speak English and came to this country with fifty dollars in his pocket, inspired me to do all I could with the gifts I had been given. That inspiration from childhood helped me realize that nothing was impossible and that I just had to prove myself and "make a difference" with each chance I was given. My humble beginning was a blessing because that lesson stayed with me throughout my career.

We can easily become disconnected in today's fast-paced environment. If we intend to thrive in this highly competitive world, we must make each moment count. No task or interaction is too small or insignificant. We can never know where an experience can take us. We must live each day believing that there are endless chances to be unique and improve everything we touch. Laurel Cutter, vice chairman of FCB Leber Katz partners, reminds us, "Your values determine your behavior. Your behavior determines your reputation, and your reputation determines your advantages."

Where IQ Meets EQ

1. Review yesterday and ask yourself, "What events, tasks, and responsibilities could I have done better?"

2. Now make the commitment to try to approach tomorrow differently and then compare the two days. Do they "feel" different?

3. What routine aspects of your life do not make a difference? How could you change them?

"Standing in the middle of the road is very dangerous; you get knocked down by traffic from both sides."

—Margaret Thatcher

Chapter

15

Choices Determine Reputation

Many conventional thinkers and commentators have stated that the beginning of the decline in ethics and morals was the point at which secularization entered the dialog. This reasoning was rooted in the fact that complex cultures and diverse communities cannot be tied down to archaic beliefs that were defined geographically hundreds of years ago. Organizations and their leaders soon became a mirror to how society was dealing with these issues and said that everything must be allowed in corporate dialog. Dr. Ravi Zacharias brilliantly deducts that the natural successor to a secularized mind-set is one that demands pluralistic options. The mandate moved from "everything goes" to "anything goes."

The moment organizations made the choice to let the code of conduct be defined by extrinsic forces, the transformation of the culture was immediate and radical. This led to privatization, where every individual in the workforce demanded a hearing for personal choices and preferences. If you have been a leader in the American workplace for the last decade, you will understand that almost every attribute of work can be challenged by someone who can claim a different preference based on politics, religion, ethnicity, or personal entitlement.

Lost in the proverbial translation of wants, needs, and the desire to belong is the recognition one needs to have about the choices we make and the chances we take. Have you ever known people who want to rebel against authority and autonomy and be for and against the same thing? How ridiculous has the desire to be free become that we actually believe that someone who takes our freedom away is a tyrant but one who tells us that bondage to ideas is good is a liberator?

G. K. Chesterton gives us a pretty good description of the skeptical nature of modern man in his book *Orthodoxy*. He says that "the new rebel is a skeptic and will not entirely trust anything. He has no loyalty; therefore, he can never be really a revolutionist. And the fact that he doubts everything really gets in his way when he wants to denounce anything." The truth we see displayed in modern workspace reveals that his assumptions of us from over a century ago are indeed true.

We have fast evolved into a culture that places undue demands on rights and not enough focus on responsibility. We consider challenging everything quite sophisticated. The conventional "out of the box" thinker is just that—one who is so desperate to change everything that he fails to realize the good buried in tradition. We have seen this approach affect people at all levels, from the school board to the halls of Congress. The goal of a hardheaded and softhearted individual is to realize that some traditions are noble and worth adhering to. The hard work of both the men to whom this book is dedicated is a perfect example of what breaking tradition represents. They held onto the highest cultural ideals that made them distinctively Italian and Indian. Yet they forced a survivalist and globalist mind-set on us, their sons, that enabled us to integrate.

Recently at a convention where I was speaking on this subject, I said to the group that modern survival requires us to abandon the stereotype that there are some places we should not go because our experience and background prevent us. Instead I said that we should stand on the periphery of accomplishment that is just out of reach and hope that the centripetal force pulls us in. This may sound like a cliché or jargon, but that is exactly how I got noticed by the late Zig Ziglar and became his closest student for almost seventeen years. There is no other way I can justify the outcome except by believing that in order to succeed, you have to integrate, and in order to integrate, you have to abandon some of the skepticism that is brought on by tradition.

The blame game seems to have reduced cultures to a spectator mind-set rather than a participative mind-set. I tried blaming my brother for all the problems he created that changed the rules when I was growing up. It did not work. I tried blaming the previous salesperson for the issues with the accounts in my assigned territory. It did not work. Now that I have a child and my own business, I realize that when we wake up, there is an "aim" frame which is optimism and a "blame" frame which is pessimism. Leadership luminary John Maxwell states that if you have been in any organization for six months, all the problems are now yours.

The myriad scenarios that confront the leaders of today are astounding. No longer can decisions on employees be made simply on productivity and talent, but we have to take into account every aspect of their identities. This task is hard but not without answers. If we are to succeed in the choices of today and tomorrow, we have to become well read in the worldviews that are defining tomorrow. No longer can we be aware of the task to do and ignorant of the people who join in the fulfillment of the task. Choose wisely, and you will win. Be WIRED for choice:

- Choose **W**isdom over Knowledge
- Choose **I**nnovation over Status Quo
- Choose **R**esponsibility over Rights
- Choose **E**mpathy over Sympathy
- Choose **D**ependability over Everything

Many of you are aware of the success of a movie called *Slumdog Millionaire*. The plot that was based on a game show and the screenplay that chronicled the life of a young boy from the slums of India and how it intersected with his answers on the game show made it a blockbuster success. One of the people who catapulted to international stardom was the man behind the music, A. R. Rahman. Many opportunities materialized in the immediate aftermath to promote the concerts and the shows of the musical maestro. Enter Victor Abraham. He decided to start an entertainment company and promote a concert. Being a new entrant into the hospitality and entertainment field, he used the best practices of others in a modular way so that he could be successful in a difficult field. Again he made a choice based on reputation to participate in something and do it well.

Although the concert in Dallas was a huge success and the reviews great, the result of his choice was evident to me almost a year later. I was speaking in India, and the organizers decided to have a musical performance before my talk. The flautist who performed was from the A. R. Rahman concert. I mentioned to him that I was involved as the MC that night in Dallas. He could not remember me but remembered the hospitality of Skypass Entertainment and being invited to Victor's home that evening. What stood out in his mind was the extra effort made to choose a good reputation over anything else.

Hardheaded and Softhearted

1. Looking at the diversity of your team, what do you still need to learn about the cultures that shape them, the languages that define them, and the history that represents them?

2. The difference between the "comfort" zone and the "effective" zone is called "growth," and

growth in some areas of life is uncomfortable. What new learning will you embark on as a choice that will seal your reputation as worldly and wise?

3. What three books will you commit to reading that will lead you to become globally diverse and universally competent?

"Wars may be fought with weapons, but they are won by men. It is the spirit of the men who follow, and of the man who leads, that gains the victory."

—**General George S. Patton**

Chapter
16

One Foot in Front of the Other

Our careers will not always go as we expect. Setbacks and failure are often a part of every endeavor or project, but we learn to face these obstacles and move through them.

Given a complex and dynamic environment, we must develop the view that whatever the setback we face, we can never allow ourselves to develop the attitude of a victim. Instead, we must learn whatever lessons exist and move on better than before. I have found that almost every successful business leader has experienced life-changing, career-altering setbacks. The distinction is not the failure, but instead the way these leaders handled the experience.

This principle also applies to a business—large or small. The ultra-competitive business environment requires constant evaluation and change—responding to things that don't work and making adjustments. The key is to develop a mission and goal that you deeply believe in and yet be willing to alter the details to find the right formula. If you believe in this mission, you should persevere because things rarely work perfectly the first time.

In 2002, I became the CEO of Quantum Corporation and faced the challenge to redefine this long-standing data storage company. The company was in a very difficult situation with most of the revenue stream declining rapidly because changing technology was taking its toll on the business. We needed to develop a growth plan to offset these declining forces. We quickly developed a strategy and went to work to diversify the revenue base. We made big acquisitions and focused on new products. We took seven years to get to the point where the company had a growth engine. Today, 70 percent of the revenue that existed in 2002 is gone and has been replaced largely by new, more profitable products in growing segments of the data storage market. The journey was difficult, and although the core mission remained the same, numerous times we redirected our programs and made course corrections. There were some very dark times, but perseverance and our willingness to learn from what didn't work made the difference.

This business lesson can be applied to our careers and lives. Accept setbacks with a willingness to evaluate the lessons learned objectively, get up, and keep moving forward. Perseverance can yield tremendous rewards and satisfaction.

One of the most surprising experiences of my career occurred in 1998. I had been in my first CEO position for a short time, and I was dealing with some very tough problems. People throughout the company were looking for answers from their new leader. Unfortunately I did not have the answers to most of the issues we were facing. Then one day I decided to get some advice.

I can remember so clearly jumping in my Jeep and driving across the valley to have lunch with another CEO who was in the middle of his own transformation. I arrived at the Apple campus and soon was sitting in the cafeteria with Steve Jobs. I figured Steve would have some sound advice on how to gain certainty and deliver a compelling vision. "What do you tell your people when they ask you about the Vision, the future?" I asked. He looked at me, puzzled, and said, "I just tell them to put one foot in front of the other."

That was it! I realized that while everyone wants clarity, vision, and assurance, real confidence comes simply from moving forward, making progress, and avoiding distractions. This was not the advice I expected, but it was a clarifying moment for me.

Where IQ Meets EQ

1. What is the mission and plan that you deeply believe in? A new career? A successful business?

2. What isn't working? What changes do you need to make?

3. Do you have setbacks that are unresolved? Do you need to internalize a lesson and move forward?

"The illiterate of the twenty-
first century will not be those
who cannot read and write but
those who cannot learn, unlearn,
and relearn."

—**Alvin Toffler**

Chapter
17

Don't Rush the Waiter for the Check

One day, rather cynically I asked Zig Ziglar why he was preparing his talk, which I personally had seen him make over four hundred times. I doubted his need to continue to prepare for something that I knew would be verbatim because he knew it well enough to deliver it from memory. His response changed everything. He told me that at that point in his life he had been considered a person of impact for over five decades, which meant that in the audience that day would be the grandson of a grandfather that Mr. Ziglar had influenced over fifty years ago. "I owe it to the grandfather's trust to be prepared for the grandson." Today when people ask me about the need for constant preparation and continuous improvement, I respond that character is defined when you practice for what will bring future rewards. Too often we are in a hurry to finish the race while still reading the book of rules.

Learning lessons has a price because we quickly realize that unlearning what does not work is sometimes harder. Here are some simple precepts to consider when embarking on a journey of lifelong lessons.

1. **Respond to constructive criticism**—The only criticism a person should worry about is the con-structive kind, for that comes out of love. The world that pays you to ply your craft has earned the right to criticize your professional output. Companies are justified in the criticism in the profit and loss exchange that is business. But the ones at home who have our better interests at heart seem to pay a heavier price than most—yet we shrug off their criticism because it's not professional. Any criticism

leveled against you should be evaluated as to whether it is constructive or destructive.

2. **Recognize destructive criticism**—Some criticism exists because the one offering it is a cynic who sees everything through the lens of pessimism. Guard yourself against people who want you to change but offer no solution. Emotional outbursts about the need for change and the desire to be hopeful about change are just platitudes. Few people accomplish anything by complaining about the previous leader or his style. Criticism should come with a proactive solution.

3. **Relax and enjoy the sunrise**—During a vacation on the Baja Peninsula, my son said that there is a new sunrise every day and that marveling at the newness with wonderment and amazement will renew your spirit. I am not asking you to look at the obvious fact that the sun will rise every day. I am asking you to recapture the wonder that comes with innocence. Looking at creation and gazing at

each new wave, while shrieking with delight when the cold waters touch your skin, is a joy that should never be lost. When we lose the innocence of wonder, we lose the joy that comes with dreaming with our eyes open.

4. **Don't rush the waiter for your check**—My bride contends that a meal shared with the ones we love has to be savored. This includes the whole experience from learning about the specials to sharing a single dessert because if everyone had an individual serving, that would be fattening. Sometimes as a family we are asked by the waiter if we need anything else because we have paid the check and are still laughing. I remember the day I dropped my son off at university. I cried more than my bride because I always thought I would have more time. I cherish the moments when we lingered after a meal but wish there were more of them.

I have learned a lot from my mentors, my bride, and my son but am constantly reminded of the moments I have squandered in my haste. Learn from your loved ones this week. Their intent is purer than your boss's memo and the next dinner you must have with that client.

Learn to listen to the least likely sources for information and wisdom that will change your outlook on becoming a lifelong learner. As you program yourself to follow the path of a career or live out the promises of a vow, stop often and ask yourself if you are doing justice to all the sources of new information. Many of the choices you make in your life will be reactionary. Learn new lessons that will allow you to be proactive so you can respond instead of react.

The bills we pay in this world are directly proportional to the things we have bought and used. When we remove "joy," "honor," "privilege," and "opportunity" from our vocabulary, we are left with a hope that someone else will solve our problems. The day we start envying what others have is the day we need a reality check because I am sure someone on planet Earth would trade places with us. Success is personal, and greed is relative—not the other way around.

My approach to learning has always been to ask those who have accomplished a lot to reveal a little about their success while not getting caught up in their fame. Recently I was on a speaking program with an entertainment icon. Just being in his presence would have been an accomplishment, and using that time to get a picture would have been opportune. I asked him a question that required him to share his wisdom. He told me that his grandfather's advice to him was that there was no amount of wealth in this world that could escape greed.

Hardheaded and Softhearted

1. As you chauffeur your kids this week, ask them questions about their lives. If something significant is happening, slow down and record it in their presence on either a digital recorder or a pocket-sized notebook.

2. What specifically will you ask your coworkers this week so that you can learn from them?

3. Who is your greatest constructive critic?

"I thank Thee first because I was never robbed before; second, because, although they took my purse they did not take my life; third, because although they took my all, it was not much; and fourth because it was I who was robbed, and not I who robbed."

—**Matthew Henry**

Chapter
18

Shortcuts and Burned Bridges

Today's business world gives the impression that we are in an "anything goes" environment where success at any cost is all that matters. I am convinced that long-term success comes only through pursuing a career based on a set of values that embraces integrity in the broadest sense. For me, integrity encompasses many elements beyond just following the law or playing by the rules. It means

- treating people, customers, and partners with respect.

- not taking shortcuts.
- neither burning bridges nor destroying relationships.
- considering all aspects when making a decision.
- being responsible to your community.
- doing what you say—meeting commitments.

I have found that this simple question—"What is the RIGHT thing to do?"—has always served me well. Whenever I have been faced with a decision, often with experts telling me what to do, I have asked myself this basic question. I have found this question to be a clarifying point in conversations that reduces all the chatter and debate to the core. Just think how different things would be if all business leaders and politicians followed this simple principle.

I definitely follow a simple principle that someone once shared with me—"one good job deserves another." These words always reinforced to me that we shouldn't allow ourselves to become wrapped up in what people think and what is popular. Instead we should do the right thing here and now. We must stay true to the belief that our long term will be good, so long as we do the present well.

I was very fortunate to have been raised in a family where integrity mattered and also to spend my formative years at Hewett-Packard while the founders were still making their mark on the company. I remember one day I was asked to come to the board meeting to explain how I was dealing with a nasty technical problem that impacted a very large number of printers that had shipped to customers and had the potential of failing. I went into the meeting with my slide deck and proceeded to explain all the ins and outs of the issue and how, although there was a huge potential for customer issues and significant cost to solve the problem, we were managing it. Then, in the middle of my discourse, Bill Hewlett asked me two piercing questions. The first was "Rick, I don't really care about all of this analysis—what is the right thing to do for our customers?" Then he followed with a second question: "What have you personally learned from this?" This was my graduate course on integrity and reputation.

Although this meeting was not my finest hour, it really changed my life. I learned to face problems and make decisions based on an enduring set of values.

Nothing is more valuable and enduring than our reputations. The most successful business leaders have taken the long view and are committed to a broad interpretation of integrity and simply "doing the right thing." This applies to every aspect of our lives—our business decisions, our relationships, and how we treat people. I believe now is the time for the business community to recommit to a business culture that places integrity as the centerpiece.

Where IQ Meets EQ

1. What relationships do you have that need repair?
2. What changes do you need to implement to make integrity a central element in your professional life?
3. What are some specific instances when you saw integrity treated as relative instead of absolute?

"Don't believe your friends when they ask you to be honest with them. All they really want is to be maintained in the good opinion they have of themselves."

—**Albert Camus**

Chapter
19

Amateurs React,
Professionals Respond

My son, Nicolas Dhanam, lay on the bed engrossed in his video game, intermittently looking up to peek at the television to ensure that he was multitasking effectively. I was at the computer, responding to a few e-mails that had come over a weekend.

One e-mail was from a participant who had seen me speak at an event and had taken offense to my tone, demeanor, substance, message, and overall presence on earth. I was trying to decide how to respond to the critical nature of the message and wondering why people take time to criticize at all. I have never seen a statue erected to critics in all my travels and hence believe they are not really held in such high esteem. Yet I was pondering the message and trying very hard to address the messenger diplomatically to convey my belief that being liked by everyone was not more important than having the pride to stand for something.

I explained to the complainer my need for self-deprecating humor and the reasons I took a few jabs at my ethnicity. I elaborately defined how the real me was actually a lot deeper in thought and intellect and asked that my humility not be overshadowed by one speech. I was actually pleading that I deserved another chance.

My son had by now moved to a position behind my right shoulder, with one eye on his game, half an eye on the television, and the other half on the e-mail on my screen. He tapped me as if to seek approval to interrupt. "What is it, boy? I am busy! I am responding to the great debate of whether I was right and a spectator was wrong. This is important stuff, and you need not be disturbing me at this time."

"Papa," he said, "I have a response to that e-mail. 'Your opinion, although interesting, is just your opinion.'" Suddenly, hope in the form of wisdom from the mouth of my progeny. My cup overflowed, for I had been bailed out not by an expert or "the system," but by that which I brought into this world. I was secure in his response for he is my son, and that definitely makes me a man. Oh, the privilege of grunting in private and gloating in public was just around the corner.

He then added his own innocent defense and said, "Papa, I heard the same speech in another venue. I was moved and told everyone I was proud of you. Now if you change it because someone who is an adult tells you to, does that mean I was wrong?" My response was mixed in that I wanted to do right by my son with one set of principles and right by the world with another set. Consistency requires a hard head and a soft heart.

On one occasion, my good friend and business partner Victor Abraham gave me some advice. He told me the difference between an amateur and a professional was often in the small things and not the big things. Victor added that in his own story of beginning with nothing and becoming a very successful entrepreneur, he realized worrying about opinions was the reaction of an amateur. Recognizing whether the opinion had merit and warranted some correction was the response of a professional

A wise man once said that if we do not stand for something, we will fall for anything. The success formula in this world adopted by some of the biggest game-changers of the last one hundred years has consistency as its cornerstone. Be consistent in all you do, and do not be swayed by the next seductive opinion and jazzy rendition. Dr. Joyce Brothers wisely observes that "You cannot consistently perform in a manner that is inconsistent with the way you see yourself."

Hardheaded and Softhearted

1. What have you altered in the face of opinion?
2. What have you changed as the public demanded because their opinions seemed greater than the private manifestations of those who love you?
3. Has another's opinion of you been greater than your opinion of yourself?

"Quality in a product or service is not what the supplier puts in. It is what the customer gets out and is willing to pay for. A product is not quality because it is hard to make and costs a lot of money, as manufacturers typically believe. This is incompetence. Customers pay only for what is of use to them and gives them value. Nothing else constitutes quality."

—Peter Drucker

Chapter
20

Finishing Well: Quality of Life, Standard of Living

The greatest tribute to a life well lived and a career that had lasting success is the finish. Often we look at the value of our accomplishments only in terms of what we have left to show for them. On the contrary, there are many more viable benchmarks that signify if your journey was indeed meritorious. The old adage that any fool can run the race but it takes a person of considerable genius to finish well holds true more now than at any other time in human history.

If you have followed the narrative of this book that showed you how to be hardheaded and softhearted by giving you the strategic formula to succeed along with the emotional foundation to cherish that success, you know that we want you to finish well. Our goal and desire to merge the ideas of corporate excellence with relational significance is designed to allow you to start, search, steer, swerve, and stop with equal finesse.

One of the people we both admire is Zig Ziglar, as evidenced by the many principles that intersected with his role as a mentor to us. His advice to us over the years of being on the speaking circuit with him was always simple and consistent. He stated that if standard of living was our number one priority, then our quality of life would never improve. He was quick to add that if quality of life was our number one priority, then standard of living was always going to improve. By following the precepts of IQ and EQ and amassing the excellence in both skill and will, you are first seeking quality of life.

After a specific activity, Zig Ziglar said, "Krish, I want you to know how proud I am of you." I was taken aback at the suddenness of the compliment, which had been delivered openly within earshot of many who would witness it. I then realized that he had chosen that moment so that he could praise me in public. I had officially been in and around the teachings of this giant of communication for almost sixteen years, and he was still praising performance. I will never forget how he was confident in demanding results but consistent in praising those that delivered those results. Here are a few behaviors to ensure finishing well:

1. **Make Your Praise Sincere**—Nothing derails a person's hopes and ambitions more than patronizing flattery that is sugarcoated. Ensure that the compliments are given at a time and in a place where the individual being lauded feels special and validated.

2. **Make Your Actions Consistent**—As the years go by, I am still speechless when my mentors call me or seek a moment with me to share ideas and processes. This consistency evokes a feeling of security in an otherwise haphazard

and chaotic world. Looking forward to those moments that have consistency as a foundation is a bonus reward in personal and professional growth.

3. **Make Your Directive Ongoing**—In the world of fast-paced ideas and ever-evolving technological changes, relationships in the workplace and in society suffer from short-term commitments. Getting educated and inspired on an ongoing basis adds to personal and professional growth.

4. **Inspect Your Expectations**—Global communication has allowed messages to travel around the world in less than two seconds, but sometimes teams within an organization seem to fall prey to lack of communication because we choose to patronize people for fear of repercussions. Learn to inspect what you expect in all you do. Your reputation determines your advantages, and sometimes we become victims of our own success by protecting the turf we inherited and not rocking the boat.

The only thing worse than communicating with your team and fostering some angst is not communicating with them and furthering ineptitude.

5. **Live by the Clock and Lead with a Vision—** Theodore Roosevelt once said that with self-discipline almost anything is possible. Today we have more time-saving devices than at any other time in human history, yet we find that more people are out of focus now than at any other time. The problem may lie in too much competition for attention. The solution lies in the simplicity of using your IQ to plan and prepare and your EQ to expect. Learn to have a few beliefs that are nonnegotiable so you can have a motivated glimpse into the wonder of tomorrow's accomplishments.

Edmund Hillary reminded us when he failed to conquer Everest on one of his attempts that the mountain had grown all it was going to grow—but that he was still growing. When he summited the peak in

1953, he put into perspective what previous failed attempts meant. He was living his day by the clock while being disciplined to tool and retool himself for success. He was also leading his life to the vision of the ultimate triumph.

If there is one lesson that needs to be recaptured today, it is about taking the long view. There are many examples of short bursts of success followed by failure. Only a truly committed person can find the balance and make sure that decisions and actions are not simply about meeting a near-term milestone at the expense of the future. Finishing strong is really about looking at the whole story, the full picture, and being able to evaluate the result in totality.

Likewise as we look back and assess our performance, we must be authentic in evaluating our achievements or lack thereof. That also includes accepting failure, which we will all experience as we navigate through this challenging environment.

I am reminded of an experience I had at Microsoft. I remember the executive team was being interviewed for a major story in one of the large national magazines. As part of the process, a reporter was interviewing the entire team and attempting to summarize how we all worked, looking for stories that would describe the interworking of the company. I was last on the list, and I can remember when the reporter came into my office and said, "Mr. Belluzzo, there is one consistent message people give about you—you are a really good person."

At first I was defensive. I didn't want to be known as "a really good person"; I wanted to be known as a hard-charging, take-no-prisoners leader. After all, that was the Microsoft culture, and I wanted to be part of the team. I worked my way through the interview, and the article was published. I now look back many years later with pride—yes, I want to be known as a really good person who can deliver results. I want to live by that advice that Dave Packard gave years ago—be hardheaded and softhearted—which I now know was not just business advice but advice on life.

Where IQ Meets EQ

1. How do you feel about your quality of life?

2. What one feature would you change to improve your quality of life as opposed to your standard of living?

3. How would your coworkers describe you? Would you be pleased with this description?

"Plan with attitude

Prepare with aptitude

Participate with servitude

Receive with gratitude

And that should be enough to

Separate you from the multitudes."

—**Krish Dhanam**

Principles of Success: Lessons from the Boardroom to the Break Room

Where IQ Meets EQ

1. **Beginning Well:** Start from the Start. Yesterday ended with last night. Today is the first day of the rest of your company. Beginning well warrants that you believe you have made a conscious effort not to let your past beat you but to let it teach you. This kind of thinking allows all your experiences to become the foundation upon which you will build a new legacy.

2. **Encouragement:** Share it, seek it, and believe it. Most of your workforce craves it. Don't make the reward and recognition just an annual affair. Encouragement is the fuel upon which hope runs, and making encouragement a culture-constant fosters proactivity in an environment that needs to change and adapt.

3. **Forces of Change:** Every culture experiences the givens of the moment, the uncontrollables of tomorrow, and the permanency of what is negotiable. Is your culture built to adapt? We all know that change is constant, but we must prepare for the change with the understanding that no longer will status quo be accepted and tolerated. Unless we have a "results rule" mentality, then IQ and EQ will not combine to produce momentum.

4. **Honesty:** Still the best policy. With integrity you have nothing to fear because you have nothing to hide. A lack of fear rising from ethical processes is liberating. A transparent leader is one who knows he is in charge and can act with the belief that he deserves to be in charge. Nothing stifles growth more than people who cannot be honest about their own abilities and qualifications to be in command.

5. **Times of Disruption:** Anticipating chaos is part of planning, and trying to avoid the

pitfalls is part of strategy. However, looking at disruption as an opportunity is unique. Great organizations have always used disruption as a signal to innovate. Some call this preparing for the opportunity that will usually reveal itself on the other side of a disruption.

6. **Addictions:** Cultures are seemingly addicted to behaviors that are counterproductive. Job security is a thing of the past. Employment security is a thing of the future. Individuals and institutions need to look at the addictive behaviors that are stifling growth and change them. Cleansing counterproductive behaviors is akin to corporate rehab.

7. **You are the Enterprise:** The three factors that characterize open and prosperous cultures are Profit, Loss, and You. Workforces that want ownership and to be included in the future of an organization should be held responsible. If merits are demanded for profitability, then there is a need for sacrifice when the enterprise is struggling.

8. **Foundations:** Nothing can be built without a solid foundation. Evaluate your culture to see who are the core people, the part-timers, the candy stripers, and the subcontractors. Each has a role, but expectations are predefined by the roles. Assessing is vital. Eliminating the lackluster performance that comes from too many people participating in nonessential roles and behaviors is a leadership opportunity.

9. **Delivering Results:** Total engagement remains the BEST model of coaching at all times: **B**elief in each as a person, **E**xpectations from each as a worker, **S**incerity in expected outcomes demanded as a partnership, and **T**ests of validity periodically to combat change.

10. **Consistency:** In a world where change is constant and innovation demanded, there is also a need for cultures to have PRIDE in the mundane. **P**ersonal **R**esponsibility **I**nstills in them a **D**esire for **E**xcellence.

11. **Be Self Aware and Open to Feedback:** Management and workers need to be told repeatedly

about the need for feedback. Every culture has to define guidelines clearly as to what is *constructive criticism* that enables improvement and what is *destructive criticism* that focuses only on the blame game. Build a culture where constructive criticism is encouraged and destructive criticism is removed.

12. **Generosity:** Having a culture that enables civic and social responsibility is a good model. Making generosity a cultural attribute will change the face of your organization in the community.

13. **Make A Difference:** Basic performance is what is expected in a job description. Expected performance is hoped for based on tools provided. Preferred performance is management utopia when the culture is constantly focused on setting new standards every year. This approach could make the attitudes in the workforce contagious and worth catching.

14. **Choices:** The founder of a half-billion-dollar company often said that we are free up to

the moment of choice, and then the choice controls the chooser. Enabling the right choices is delicate, and studying companies that have consistently allowed their employees to make the right choices for generations is an eye-opening look into reality.

15. **It's a Journey:** Thinking that the steady, consistent performer will finish best is not a fable. The prop used by Zig Ziglar to conclude some speeches was an old fashioned water pump. He indicated that before you begin, you have to prime the pump. Then the greater the quality of the water, the deeper the well will be—and the more difficult the initial effort.

Once the approach is secure and the steps followed, all you have to do is maintain an easy, steady pace for the best reward. Any journey warrants a beginning and an ending, but in the neutral zone of travel, decisions of destiny are made.

16. **Learning:** Learning cultures invest in the future needs of their present employees so that

past performance is not the only indicator for advancement. Bench planning and talent management are necessary for grooming new leaders. A learning culture creates a road map for all employees.

17. **Integrity:** If honesty is a policy, then integrity is the measurement that honest and ethical approaches are being followed. By establishing guidelines to inspect what you expect, you will create a culture that focuses on integrity in all employees.

18. **Opinions:** Most organizations treat work flow in terms of specific guidelines for process compatibility and executing excellence. However, by equating the output of one series of work processes to the input of another's effectiveness, you create continuity. Changing opinions about work in general will enable a culture to perform on autopilot but with the necessary motivation not to consider it robotic.

19. **Service:** The organizational iceberg has two components: the visible external customers

who are overt and the invisible internal customers who are covert. While we can gauge the effectiveness of the product or service by looking at the satisfaction index of the external customers, we cannot necessarily gauge the same about the internal customers. Policy should reflect that both external and internal customers are vital and that service excellence should be recognized and rewarded at all levels in the service chain.

20. **Expansion:** Being penny-wise and pound-foolish has limited the opportunity for growth. True expansion for a culture requires the ability to create short-term goals, medium-range ambitions, and long-term visions. One allows activity to relate to the second through mission and arrive at the third by execution.

21. **Finishing Well:** Shareholders and stake holders are the ultimate authority on the success of an enterprise. Knowing that you finished well is possible only when you create some nonnegotiable aspects of your business. The

organization that makes its cause bigger than its ego allows itself to work for progress and not perfection. This continuous improvement will allow your culture to finish well regardless of whether your business model was modular, without boundaries, or virtual.

About the Authors

Rick Belluzzo has spent his entire thirty six year career in the technology industry, most of it building innovative new product categories and leading companies through change. Most recently he served as Chairman and CEO of Quantum Corporation, where he led the company through a transition from a storage device company to a company which specializes in corporate data management and protection.

Before joining Quantum, Belluzzo held senior management positions with Microsoft Corporation, most recently President and COO. Before that, he led the Consumer Group, which was responsible for products such as Xbox. Prior to Microsoft, he was CEO of Silicon Graphics, Inc.

His career in technology began at Hewlett-Packard, which he joined in 1975 after earning a BS in accounting and finance from Golden Gate University. During his twenty-three years at HP, Belluzzo held several key leadership positions including VP of the printer and PC business as well as Executive VP of the computer organization.

Currently he serves on several boards and invests and consults with early-stage companies. He frequently conducts seminars and speaks on leadership and change.

Krish Dhanam was born in India. In 1984, he finished his MBA at the Institute of Management Technology and migrated to the United States with his bride, Anila. Winning a sales contest in 1990 earned him a ticket to a seminar conducted by the legendary motivator Zig Ziglar. This chance encounter would be the catalyst that shaped the next two decades as Krish joined the Ziglar Corporation in 1991 as a telemarketer and eventually became the vice president of global operations.

Through training, teaching, and facilitating seminars all over the world, Krish launched his professional speaking career. As one of only two executive coaches personally trained by Zig Ziglar, Krish has successfully delivered his message of hope, humor, and balance in over fifty countries and throughout the continental United States. As a curriculum designer, he has authored programs on staff development, sales, leadership, personal development, and communication. His client list is the who's who of global enterprise, and he has received accolades from some of the most distinguished organizations, including the United States Army, Christian Dior, Steelcase Industries, Apollo Hospitals, Electronic Data Systems, Texas Instruments, PepsiCo, and Energizer Batteries.

Today he continues to serve as the global ambassador for the Ziglar group of companies. He is the cofounder of his own training company and author of *The American Dream from an Indian Heart* and *From Abstracts to Absolutes*. He is also a contributing author to *Top Performance* by Zig Ziglar.

He serves on the board of the Ravi Zacharias Life Focus Society and Life Focus Knowledge Ventures Pvt. Ltd. in India. He is also the brand ambassador for www.GoAmbition.com and managing partner at SkyLife Success.